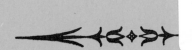

Roy Campbell

by DAVID WRIGHT

Published for The British Council
and The National Book League
by Longmans, Green & Co.

Two shillings and sixpence net

Roy Campbell was born in 1901 in Natal, and died in Portugal, after a life of great variety and achievement. In this essay Mr. Wright assesses Campbell's work in poetry and prose. He justly says that 'he affirmed, in his life and in his work, the validity of the poetic vocation, its serious character and its morality of delight, in an age when its existence is either denied or, by pedants and cultural organisations, polluted by various subtle and well meant forms of standardisation and commercialism'.

Mr. Wright was born in South Africa and has published several books of poetry, including *Monologue of a Deaf Man*. He is one of the editors of *X*, a quarterly review of literature and art.

Thanks are due to Messrs. The Bodley Head Ltd. for allowing the use of quotation from the volumes of *Collected Poems* by Roy Campbell; to Messrs. Jonathan Cape for quotations from *The Flaming Terrapin* and *The Wayzgoose*; to Mrs. Mary Campbell for quotations from *Adamastor*; to Messrs. Faber & Faber for quotations from *Talking Bronco*, and to Messrs. The Harvill Press for quotations from Roy Campbell's translation of the work of St. John of the Cross.

Bibliographical Series
of Supplements to 'British Book News'
on Writers and Their Work

★

GENERAL EDITOR
Bonamy Dobrée

¶ Roy Campbell was born in 1901 in Natal. He died in Portugal on 23 April 1957.

ROY CAMPBELL

from a photograph by JANE BOWN
reproduced by courtesy of The Observer

ROY
CAMPBELL

by

DAVID WRIGHT

PUBLISHED FOR
THE BRITISH COUNCIL
and the NATIONAL BOOK LEAGUE
by LONGMANS, GREEN & CO.

LONGMANS, GREEN & CO. LTD.
48 Grosvenor Street, London W.1
Thibault House, Thibault Square, Cape Town
605–611 Lonsdale Street, Melbourne, C.1

LONGMANS, GREEN & CO. INC.
119 West 40th Street, New York 18

LONGMANS, GREEN & CO.
20 Cranfield Road, Toronto 16

ORIENT LONGMANS LTD.
Calcutta Bombay Madras
Delhi Hyderabad Dacca

Printed in Great Britain by
F. Mildner & Sons, London, E.C.1

ROY CAMPBELL

I

Aᴌᴛʜᴏᴜɢʜ he spent the best part of his life in Europe, in either England, France, Spain, or Portugal, Roy Campbell is quite properly regarded as the first South African poet of real eminence. It is primarily his South African birth and half-pastoral upbringing that gives his work its unique bias. Yet his poetry is in no way parochial, for at a time when most of his English contemporaries, apart from Pound and Eliot, were doggedly thumbing Wordsworth and Tennyson, the young South African found his way to the great European Romantics, to Rimbaud, Baudelaire, and even Valéry. In Campbell, many contradictory, not to say paradoxical, elements are juxtaposed. Some have remarked that he was a man born out of his time, who would have been happier in a more flamboyant era like that of the first Elizabeth; yet with equal justice it can be said that he was more at home in the twentieth century than most poets who were his contemporaries. These have, generally speaking, led retired, almost eighteenth-century, lives in an age notable for world wars, revolutions, and an unprecedented proliferation of mechanical invention. But Campbell's passion for actuality and experience drove him to sample almost every kind of sensation the present century affords (he piloted gliders and speedboats, was expert with motor-bicycles as well as horses, hunted with the gun as well as the spear, and even, towards the end of his life, took up skin-diving). It also involved him in two of its wars. At different periods he made his living as a bull-fighter, fisherman, horse-trader, and BBC producer. Yet in spite of these activities there was in him an element of mysticism, which enabled the satirist who wrote *The Georgiad* and the violent polemics of *Flowering Rifle* to produce an unequalled translation of the visionary poems of St. John of the Cross. Like Byron, Campbell was a man of action; and, like Byron's, Campbell's literary output was copious and uneven. Before his death, at 56, he had published two fat volumes of collected verse. He had translated the whole of the poems of Baudelaire, and of St. John of the Cross, most of the verse of Frederico Garcia Lorca (though the bulk of this is still unpublished), a number of plays by Spanish dramatists, such as Lope de Vega and Tirso de Molina, two novels by the Portuguese, Eça de Quieroz, and much Portuguese poetry, and many isolated poems of Rimbaud, Valéry, Quevedo, Gongora and Camoës. He had also written five or six prose books, including two autobiographies and a study of Lorca.

Roy Campbell was born in 1901, in Natal. At that time Natal was a British colony, the only province, in what became the Union of South Africa, to have been settled originally by the British (the others were founded by Dutch colonists or Boer trekkers). His forebears had been among the early settlers of Natal; they were of Irish extraction, and an eighteenth-century ancestor was said to have been a fiddler and a ballad-singer from Donegal. In Durban (where the poet was born) the Campbell family enjoyed considerable local importance. Campbell's father, a well-known doctor who helped to found the Natal Technical College and the Howard University of Durban, was a scholar, and a friend of many notable people, among them the American humorist Mark Twain. On Campbell's mother's side ran Highland and also, perhaps significantly, Gascon blood; his maternal grandfather, a Scottish laird, had known Browning, Tennyson, Rossetti, and other Pre-Raphaelites.

The South Africa in which Campbell grew up bore little resemblance to the one that now exists. At that period

Durban was a small port largely dependent on its whaling industry; and game, now shot off except in the vicinity of the reserves, remained prolific in most parts of Natal. The Campbell family owned a cottage on a lagoon in the wilds, where their children learned to ride, fish and shoot; holidays were spent with cousins in Rhodesia (then almost virgin bush) on long ox-wagon expeditions in the traditional trekker style, hunting impala, sable, kudu, and the scores of varieties of antelope and big game with which the country then abounded. Some idea has to be given of Campbell's background and upbringing if the cast of his mind is to be understood; and, in particular, it is necessary to emphasize the fact that the South Africa in which he was brought up had yet to experience its Industrial Revolution. And because Campbell's ancestors (as he often remarked) had 'cleared out of Britain at the first whiff of the nineteenth century', Campbell's own angle of view of the modern world was not conditioned by familiarity with its demagogic pollutions but remained that of a bucolic pre-Victorian:

> who never was put through any mill except that of the pre-Industrial European culture of an equestrian, slightly feudal type, a sort of inhabitant of the moon, a foreign being who cannot imagine what meaning such words as 'rights', 'progress', 'freedom', and 'liberty' have at all . . .The dehumanization of Europe is contemporaneous with the currency of these words.
>
> (*Broken Record*)

Against that 'dehumanization', the Romantic Movement of the nineteenth century was, in a sense, a protest and a revolt. Campbell was a Romantic in the serious sense of the word, in that he was of the line of Romantics like Stendhal and Baudelaire, who upheld the individual, the personal, and the value of the imaginative and intuitive faculties, in the face of technicism, standardization, 'progress', bureaucratization, and the menace of the anonymous millions,

Who have no purpose save to multiply,
Who have no will save all to be the same
(*A Song for the People*)

the menace of what Ortega y Gasset calls 'the commonplace mind, knowing itself to be commonplace, that has the
assurance to proclaim the rights of the commonplace and
impose it wherever it will'. Generic to nineteenth-century
Romantics like Baudelaire, and to their descendants of the
twentieth century, e.g. Henri de Montherlant, Wyndham
Lewis, and Campbell himself, has been a contempt of
mediocrity and a distrust of 'democracy', both of which
they saw as different aspects of the same corruption.

Because Campbell held these anti-liberal views and lived
in the twentieth instead of the nineteenth century, he laid
himself open to the accusation (as did de Montherlant,
Wyndham Lewis, Ezra Pound, and even, to a less extent,
W. B. Yeats and T. S. Eliot) of being Fascist. While Campbell
believed society should be hierarchic, he valued the indivi-
dual, but suspected the catchword slogans of demagoguery:
'I hate Humanity and all such abstracts; but I love *people*.'
In fact Campbell abhorred totalitarian systems, whether
Fascist or Communist, and opposed both, though not,
unfortunately for him, in the fashionable order. During the
Spanish Civil War (which, having recently become a
Roman Catholic, he regarded as a Christian crusade against
Communism) he supported Franco's side. But at that time
socialism exercised a strong emotional appeal among most
intellectuals, who saw the conflict wholly as a struggle
between democracy and totalitarian Fascism represented by
Franco, especially when Franco accepted military aid from
Hitler and Mussolini. On this account, the image of Campbell
as some sort of Fascist was never quite got rid of, even though
he was later one of the few poets of his generation to serve
in arms against the Fascists in the second world war.

As in the case of Baudelaire, and those other Romantic
poets and writers who, reacting to the first wave of the
Industrial Revolution, found themselves at loggerheads with

materialism, liberal progressiveness, and the accepted 'advanced' thought of their time, Campbell's life and personality are not to be disentangled from his poetry if a proper conspectus is to be obtained. It is no accident that there was an element of Dandyism, spiritual and sartorial, in Campbell, as well as in Byron and Baudelaire; though in each case, of course, it took a different form. Significantly, the word 'Dandy' came into currency about the same time as the beginning of the Industrial Revolution, which inaugurated the era of the masses, of Ortega's Mass-man who 'crushes beneath [him] everything that is different, everything that is excellent, individual, qualified and select. Anybody who is not like everybody, who does not think like everybody, runs the risk of being eliminated . . . The mass is all that which sets no value on itself—good or ill— on specific grounds, but which feels itself "*just like everybody*".' The Dandy, on the other hand, asserts in dress and in behaviour his uniqueness, his individuality, and his personality, in the face of the herd. He is not a 'bohemian': for bohemians merely express their nonconformity, which is, in itself, a form of conformity; bohemian dress and behaviour being as uniform as the conventional clothes and manners it replaces. Campbell's Dandyism came out in a kind of braggadocio, in which he paraded his abilities as a frontiersman, bullfighter, equestrian; that is to say precisely those attributes least associated with the conventional type of aesthete. Whereas the poets who were his contemporaries mostly dressed and behaved like stockbrokers, Campbell flaunted a colonial Stetson or a black Spanish cordoba, and, in addition, an apparent readiness to settle literary disputes with his fist as well as his pen. While the boisterous panache of Campbell's personality and behaviour can easily be dismissed as exhibitionism (as the diabolism of Baudelaire was by his contemporaries) it might be nearer the truth to see it as a romantic mask, deliberately assumed, to challenge accepted attitudes and the bovine acquiescence of the majority to the values of the herd.

II

It was in 1918, in the last year of the war whose outbreak had signalled the extinction of the nineteenth century in Europe, that Campbell left South Africa. Arrived in England, he went to Oxford as a student. He never actually entered the University, but though his stay in Oxford was brief (not more than a twelvemonth), it proved crucial. While there he formed a friendship with the composer William Walton, through whom he met some of those writers and artists who constituted the real avant-garde of the time: Wyndham Lewis (the editor of *Blast*), T. S. Eliot, the Sitwells, and Thomas Earp. Earp's influence was decisive. He took Campbell with him to Paris (this was the beginning of Campbell's lifelong affection for France) and introduced him to the poems of Rimbaud and Paul Valéry, the latter being then little known in England.

At this period Campbell was still in his teens and already writing poetry, none of which has survived. According to his autobiography, most of these poems were about railway-stations (to him unfamiliar and fascinating phenomena) and imitative of the early Eliot. Certainly there was nothing remotely resembling the conversational cadences, compression, and incisive ambiguity of *The Love Song of J. Alfred Prufrock* in Campbell's first published work. This was *The Flaming Terrapin*, which appeared in 1924 and immediately created a literary sensation.

It was the energy and flamboyance of *The Flaming Terrapin* that surprised everyone. Its verve and extravagance burst like a bomb in the middle of the faded prettiness of the 'Georgian' poetry then in vogue. Written in conventionally rhyming iambic pentameters, it was obviously not 'modernist' in the manner of Pound, Eliot or the Sitwells, yet in everything else appeared far removed from the fatigued 'traditionalism' of the 'Georgians'. Epigoni of the Victorian poetic achievement, the 'Georgians' (a group with which poets like J. C. Squire, Robert Nichols, John Drinkwater, and John Freeman were then associated) based their technique on the sugary metres and diction of the nineteenth century. But the new arrival evidently owed much to the muscular heroic couplets employed by Dryden and Pope, who were, in those days, not only out of fashion but even considered unpoetic. Campbell's flamboyant imagery, drawn from his memories of the spectacular and bizarre vegetation and fauna of his native Africa, exploded with an almost surrealist proliferation and exoticism. Today, it is not so easy to appreciate the impact made by this long and rambling poem, which at one stroke established Campbell, at the age of twenty-three, as a poet of achievement rather than promise. Its rhythms and imagery seem turgid and confused; there is a noticeable repetitiousness of effect. The impression is left of muddled power, of an unchannelled forcefulness and energy; for all the novelty of its images, *The Flaming Terrapin* remains very much a young man's poem, a hyperbolic conglomerate of Shelley, Byron, and Keats, served up on a structural basis of homemade Pope-and-Dryden. But, as a contemporary reviewer noted in *The Times Literary Supplement*, the poem 'evokes exotic landscape in the same way as the central stanzas of *Bateau Ivre* ... it is probably the first instance of the influence of Rimbaud in English verse'.

Campbell called his poem a 'symbolic vision of the salvation of civilization'. It describes the launching of Noah's Ark (representing the created world under the dominion of man) whose subsequent voyage during the Flood, towed by a giant terrapin (symbolizing energy) through a series of fantastic, semi-apocalyptic set-scenes—reminiscent of those grandiloquent engravings by John Martin that used to illustrate Victorian editions of *Paradise Lost*—is threatened at different points by various personified abstractions (Anarchy, Mediocrity, Patriotism, Corruption). In the poem, Campbell strikes an attitude which was to prove idiosyncratic:

> Far be the bookish Muses! Let them find
> Poets more spruce, and with pale fingers bind
> The bays in garlands for their northern kind.
> My task demands a virgin muse to string
> A lyre of savage thunder as I sing.

But *The Flaming Terrapin* remains notable for its scattered passages of authentic poetry; for example the remarkable and finely-observed image of Corruption descending on the cities of the world

> with movements as of one
> Who, diving after pearls, down from the sun
> Along the shaft of his own shadow slides
> With knife in grinning jaws; and as he glides,
> Nearing the twilight of the nether sands,
> Under him swings his body deft and slow,
> Gathers his knees up, reaches down his hands
> And settles on his shadow like a crow.

III

An act of unconscious literary tutelage may be said to have been performed when the third mate of the cargo-boat in which the young Campbell worked his passage to England, pushed the poet's copies of Pope and Dryden out of the port-hole with the remark, 'They'll never get you anywhere'. *The Flaming Terrapin* had no rigid rhyme-scheme, but contained long stretches of heroic couplets modelled on those of Dryden. Campbell's next poem, *The Wayzgoose*, a satire, was written entirely in this metre. Not surprisingly, its style leaned even more heavily on Dryden's *MacFlecknoe* and Pope's *Dunciad*. Later Campbell was to write two other long poems, *The Georgiad* and *Flowering Rifle*, also in heroic couplets. While Campbell had force and humour, and was ingenious at producing original and often witty rhymes, and while his diction was racy and colloquial and nearly always vivid and alive, he did not have the subtlety of ear which the manipulation of this metre requires, nor could he manage the delicate variations of pace and beat with which Dryden and Pope were able to elude monotony, the chief peril of the form. Worse, writing in heroic couplets encouraged Campbell's great weakness, a tendency to the prolix; and it may be said here and now all his poems in this metre suffer from monotony and go on far too long.

Campbell's first satiric poem, *The Wayzgoose* (the title comes from the name given to an annual outing or bean-feast of printers and their employees) arose out of his return to South Africa where, with William Plomer and Laurens van der Post, in 1928 he founded and edited *Voorslag*, the first literary magazine, or 'little review', to appear in that country. His editorship of *Voorslag* lasted no more than a couple of numbers, for the magazine upset local susceptibilities by attacking the colour-bar, while a story of Plomer's that appeared in its pages was considered pornographic. In the course of the subsequent ructions, Campbell and his associates resigned, after which the review soon folded up. To these events, Campbell reacted with *The Wayzgoose*, a venomously funny exposé of South African prejudices and parochialism and of the local pretensions to culture. It opened with a bang:

> Attend my fable if your ears be clean,
> In fair Banana Land we lay our scene—
> South Africa, renowned both far and wide
> For politics and little else beside:
> Where, having torn the land with shot and shell,
> Our sturdy pioneers as farmers dwell,
> And, twixt the hours of strenuous sleep, relax
> To sheer the fleeces or to fleece the blacks . . .

The local and topical allusions in *The Wayzgoose* make parts of it obscure to readers who have no specialized knowledge of South African politics of three decades ago; but there are passages in it that seem even more relevant today than they were when Campbell set them down:

> This is the ultimatum that you shirk,
> The awful question—Poverty or Work?
> Work, that can turn a draper to a Man
> And give the human accident a plan . . .
> Is it the sign of a 'superior race'
> To whine to have 'the nigger kept in place'?
> Where is his place save in his strength and sense,
> And will he stand aside for impotence,
> Does Evolution wait for those who lag
> Or curtsy to a cheap colonial Flag?
> Is this 'White Labour'—lolling on this stool,
> Fed by a black with every needful tool,
> The white man sits and uses but his hands,
> The black man does the thinking while he stands.

The technique of boisterous ridicule, which Campbell first used in *The Wayzgoose*, was developed and more successfully employed in a shorter satiric piece, *A Veld Eclogue*, written about the same time but published much later. Here he makes fun of the sentimental colonial writers of the period:

> Who tell us plainly that the world's more wide
> On the colonial than the other side. . .
> And there are far more furlongs to the mile
> In Africa than Europe—though no doubt
> None but colonials have found this out . . .
> Nobody can deny that our hills rise
> Far more majestically—for their size!
> I mean that there is something grander, yes,
> About the veld, than I can well express,
> Something more vast—perhaps I don't mean that—
> Something more round, and square, and steep, and flat—
> No, well perhaps it's not quite that I mean
> But something, rather, half-way in between,

Something more 'nameless'—That's the very word!
Something that can't be felt, or seen, or heard,
Or even thought—a kind of mental mist
That doesn't either matter or exist
But without which it would go very hard
With many a local novelist and bard—
Being the only trick they've ever done,
To bring in local colour where there's none:
And if I introduce the system too,
Blame only the traditions I pursue.

Veld Eclogue appeared in *Adamastor* in 1930. At this period,
Campbell, having left South Africa for good (except for one
or two visits that he made during and after the second world
war) was living in the South of France, supporting himself
alternately as a bullfighter and a fisherman. He felt at home
among the cattlemen and cowboys of Provence, where
the landscape was reminiscent of Africa but had the advantage
of having been moulded by European civilization and
culture. *Adamastor* is the first and best collection of Campbell's
poems, for besides containing the cream of his satire and
most of his finest lyrics, it includes key pieces like *Horses
on the Camargue* and *Tristan da Cunha*, in which he gives
eloquent expression to his central beliefs. His sharpest
epigrams appear in this book, including the famous:

On Some South African Novelists

You praise the firm restraint with which they write,
I'm with you there, of course.
They use the snaffle and the curb all right—
But where's the bloody horse?

And:

*The Land Grabber:
On a Poet who Offered his Heart for a
Handful of South African Soil*

The bargain is fair and the bard is no robber,
A handful of dirt for a heartful of slobber.

As a satirist, Campbell is at his best in brief epigrams like these, for he nearly always spoiled his lengthier satires because he could not resist going on long after his point had been made. His more ambitious satirical works seldom achieve the compressed savagery of, for example, the four lines of the epigram entitled *Holism* (the name of a philosophical work published by General Smuts some time after two Native villages had been wiped out, one of them for failing to pay a dog-tax, during his Premiership of South Africa):

> The love of Nature burning in his heart,
> Our new Saint Francis offers us his book—
> The saint that fed the birds at Bondleswaart
> And fattened up the vultures at Bull Hoek.

IV

Adamastor contains a number of poems which are central to the understanding of Campbell in that they define his romantic attitude and make explicit his concept of the poet as a heroic and isolated figure, an Ishmael from the wilderness. In one of the finest of them, this is indirectly expressed by means of the image of the wild horses in the Camargue marshes:

> Theirs is no earthly breed
> Who only haunt the verges of the earth
> And only on the sea's salt herbage feed . . .
>
> . . . Still out of hardship bred,
> Spirits of power and beauty and delight
> Have ever on such frugal pastures fed
> And loved to course with tempests through the night.
> (*Horses on the Camargue*)

The theme is restated in a rehandling of the subject of one of Byron's poems, *Mazeppa*, in which the naked youth

bound to the back of a wild horse driven into the desert,
survives the ordeal to become a Cossack king:

And so it is, whenever some new god,
Boastful, and young, and avid of renown,
Would make his presence known upon the earth—
Choosing some wretch from those of mortal birth
He takes his body like a helpless clod
And on the croup of genius straps it down . . .

Out of his pain, perhaps, some god-like thing
Is born. A god has touched him, though with whips:
We only know that, hooted from our walls,
He hurtles on his way, he reels, he falls,
And staggers up to find himself a king
With truth a silver trumpet at his lips.

Again there is his image of the poet as 'a restive steer', a
lawbreaker expelled from the protection of the herd:

The Making of a Poet

In every herd there is some restive steer
Who leaps the cows and heads each hot stampede,
Till the old bulls unite in jealous fear
To hunt him from the pastures where they feed.

Lost in the night he hears the jungles crash
And desperately, lest his courage fail,
Across his hollow flanks with sounding lash
Scourges the heavy whipcord of his tail.

Far from the phalanxes of horns that ward
The sleeping herds he keeps the wolf at bay,
At nightfall by the slinking leopard spoored,
And goaded by the fly-swarm through the day.

More than once Campbell uses the snake (which lives among
rocks and is solitary in its habits) to symbolize the poet whose

> clear unchanging sight
> Through triumph, change, decay,
> In such a serpent's coiled repose
> His secret architecture knows.
>   (*The Snake*)

Or:

> Our lonely lives in every chance agreeing,
> It is no common friendship that you bring,
> It was the desert starved us into being
> The hate of men that sharpened us to sting:
> Sired by starvation, suckled by neglect,
> Hate was the surly tutor of our youth:
> I too can hiss the hair of men erect
> Because my lips are venomous with truth.
>   (*To a Pet Cobra*)

Since the nineteenth century, poets have tended to be obsessed with the isolated situation of the poet in modern society, where his purpose and values have become increasingly disparate from its desires and price-tags. Baudelaire expressed the arrogance, isolation, and vulnerability of that position in the famous sonnet in which he drew an analogy between the albatross tormented by its captors and the situation of the poet. This was, perhaps not surprisingly, the first of Baudelaire's poems to be translated by Campbell:

> The Poet, like this monarch of the clouds,
> Despising archers, rides the storm elate.
> But, stranded on the earth to jeering crowds,
> The great wings of the giant baulk his gait.
>   (*The Albatross*)

Tristan da Cunha is the poem in which Campbell expressed his own sense of isolation and exile, both as a poet and as a man. While not as perfect as some of his shorter pieces (*The Sisters*, or *The Zulu Girl* for instance) it is weightier, more personal, and deeply felt. Without comparing the two poems, one may say that *Tristan da Cunha* stands in something of the same relation to Campbell as that far greater poem *Resolution and Independence* (in which the altered circumstances of the poet, in all its insecurity and isolation, to a society inimical or indifferent to his existence and purpose is faced) does to Wordsworth. Tristan da Cunha is Campbell's Leech-Gatherer. As a young man Campbell had seen the island from the deck of a Durban whaler. Campbell's imagination transformed this remote storm-beaten rock

> Hurled by what aim to what tremendous range!
> A missile from the great sling of the past

into an emblem of the poet, solitary, anachronistic, and disdainful:

> Around your rocks you furl the shawling snow
> Half-sunk in your own darkness, vast and grim,
> And round you on the deep with surly motion
> Pivot your league-long shadow as you swim.
>
> Why should you haunt me thus but that I know
> My surly heart is in your own displayed,
> Round whom such leagues in endless circuit flow,
> Whose hours in such a gloomy compass run—
> A dial with its league-long arm of shade
> Slowly revolving to the moon and sun.
>
> My pride has sunk, like your grey fissured crags,
> By its own strength o'ertoppled and betrayed:
> I, too, have burned the wind with fiery flags
> Who now am but a roost for empty words,
> An island of the sea whose only trade
> Is in the voyages of its wandering birds.
>
> . . . Exiled like you and severed from my race
> By the cold ocean of my own disdain,
> Do I not freeze in such a wintry space,
> Do I not travel through a storm as vast,
> And rise at times, victorious from the main
> To fly the sunrise at my shattered mast?

Your path is but a desert where you reap
Only the bitter knowledge of your soul:
You fish with nets of seaweed in the deep
As fruitlessly as I with nets of rhyme—
Yet forth you stride, yourself the way, the goal,
The surges are your strides, your path is time.

. . . We shall not meet again; over the wave
Our ways divide, and yours is straight and endless,
But mine is short and crooked to the grave:
Yet what of these dark crowds amidst whose flow
I battle like a rock, aloof and friendless,
Are not their generations vague and endless,
The waves, the strides, the feet on which I go?

V

In *Adamastor* are to be found some of Campbell's most
perfect lyrics, *The Serf*, *The Zulu Girl*, *The Zebras*, and *The
Sisters*. The point to note about the last three is Campbell's
authority in the manipulation of images, and the sureness
with which he transforms what might otherwise have been
mere set-pieces of descriptive writing into valid depositions
of the imagination, yet without dragging in some tag-end
'moral'. *The Zulu Girl* and *The Sisters* are notable instances.
All these poems are on South African themes and show the
influence of Rimbaud, particularly *The Zulu Girl*, which
obviously owes something to *Les Chercheuses de Poux* (The
Louse Pickers). It is deservedly one of Campbell's best-known
poems:

When in the sun the hot red acres smoulder,
Down where the sweating gang its labour plies,
A girl flings down her hoe, and from her shoulder
Unslings her child tormented by the flies.

She takes him to a ring of shadow pooled
By thorn-trees: purpled with the blood of ticks,
While her sharp nails, in slow caresses ruled,
Prowl through his hair with sharp electric clicks,

His sleepy mouth plugged by the heavy nipple,
Tugs like a puppy, grunting as he feeds:
Through his frail nerves her own deep langours ripple,
Like a broad river sighing through the reeds.

Yet in that drowsy stream his flesh imbibes
An old unquenched unsmotherable heat—
The curbed ferocity of beaten tribes,
The sullen dignity of their defeat.

Her body looms above him as a hill
Within whose shade a village lies at rest,
Or the first cloud so terrible and still
That bears the coming harvest in its breast.

In the sonnet called *The Zebras*, he combines energy with
exotic sensuousness in a series of brilliant images, so that
while evoking lushness the poem itself contains none:

From the dark woods that breathe of fallen showers,
Harnessed with level rays in golden reins,
The zebras draw the dawn across the plains
Wading knee-deep among the scarlet flowers.
The sunlight, zithering their flanks with fire,
Flashes between the shadows as they pass,
Barred with electric tremors through the grass
Like wind across the gold strings of a lyre.

Into the flushed air snorting rosy plumes
That smoulder round their feet in drifting fumes,
With dove-like voices call the distant fillies,
While round the herds the stallion wheels his flight,
Engine of beauty volted with delight,
To roll his mare among the trampled lilies.

The Sisters probably bears the greatest debt to Rimbaud yet shows the least direct evidence of that influence. As in the case of the other two, the poem is apparently no more than description of an incident, but Campbell, especially in the last stanza, exercises a superb mastery in the selection and deployment of images to produce that reverberation of latent implication which is one of the *raisons d'etre* of poetry:

> After hot loveless nights, when cold winds stream
> Sprinkling the frost and dew, before the light,
> Bored with the foolish things that girls must dream
> Because their beds are empty of delight,
>
> Two sisters rise and strip. Out from the night
> Their horses run to their low-whistled pleas—
> Vast phantom shapes with eyeballs rolling white
> That sneeze a fiery steam about their knees:
>
> Through the crisp manes their stealthy prowling hands,
> Stronger than curbs, in slow caresses rove,
> They gallop down across the milk-white sands
> And wade far out into the sleeping cove:
>
> The frost stings sweetly with a burning kiss
> As intimate as love, as cold as death:
> Their lips, whereon delicious tremors hiss,
> Fume with the ghostly pollen of their breath.
>
> Far out on the grey silence of the flood
> They watch the dawn in smouldering gyres expand
> Beyond them: and the day burns through their blood
> Like a white candle through a shuttered hand.

Here, it may be remarked that Campbell's most striking images owe their effectiveness to a precision and accuracy of observation even where they seem most rhetorically 'poetic'. The comparison of the Zulu girl's breast to

> the first cloud so terrible and still
> That bears the coming harvest on its breast

while carrying the obvious implication, (of the resentment of a defeated race and threat of its awakening, the whirlwind yet to be reaped) also conveys an exact impression of the kind of thundercloud that in Africa brings the first rains after the long drought. It is this fidelity to the specific that gives his metaphors resonance and weight. Were Campbell's images not shot through with an authentic attention to reality, lines like 'The zebras draw the dawn across the plains' would have an effect of inflated poeticality instead of succeeding as they do.

This quality rescues the sensuous romanticism of *Choosing a Mast* (one of the best poems in *Flowering Reeds*, the collection that succeeded *Adamastor*) from the voluptuous squashiness into which a writer less involved with actuality might have allowed it to drift. All good poems hover on the verge of being bad ones; and perhaps it is the tension created thereby (like watching a performer on a tightrope) that partly accounts for their succeeding. In many ways *Choosing a Mast* is the most typical of Campbell's poems, and its first and last stanzas should be quoted here:

> This mast, new-shaved, through whom I rive the ropes,
> Says she was once an oread of the slopes,
> Graceful and tall upon the rocky highlands,
> A slender tree as vertical as noon,
> And her low voice was lovely as the silence
> Through which a fountain whistles to the moon,
> Who now of her white spray must take the veil
> And, for her songs, the thunder of the sail. . .
>
> . . . Under a pine, when summer days were deep,
> We loved the most to lie in love or sleep:
> And when in long hexameters the west
> Rolled his grey surge, the forest for his lyre,
> It was the pines that sang us to our rest.
> Loud in the wind and fragrant in the fire,
> With legioned voices swelling all night long,
> From Pelion to Provence, their storm of song.

It was the pines that fanned us in the heat,
The pines, that cheered us in the time of sleet,
For which sweet gifts I set one dryad free:
No longer to the wind a rooted foe,
This nymph shall wander where she longs to be
And with the blue north wind arise and go,
A silver huntress with the moon to run
And fly through rainbows with the rising sun;

And when to pasture in the glittering shoals
The guardian mistral drives his thundering foals,
And when like Tartar horsemen racing free
We ride the snorting fillies of the sea,
My pine shall be the archer of the gale
While on the bending willow curves the sail
From whose great bow the long keel shooting home
Shall fly, the feathered arrow of the foam.

VI

At the time when the poems in *Flowering Reeds* and
the later collection, *Mithraic Emblems*, were being written,
Campbell was leading a life of action in the South of France.
He became well-known as a *razeteur* (bullfighter in the
Provençal version of the sport, in which the bull is not
killed: the *razeteur* has to try to seize the cocarde worn
between its horns). It was about this period that he became
a Roman Catholic. As with the French playwright and
novelist Henri de Montherlant, also a toreador, bullfighting, which especially in its Spanish form is more a
ritual than a sport, brought out the vein of mysticism latent
in Campbell. This found some expression in the series of
emblematic poems called *Mithraic Frieze*, of which *To the
Sun* is a specimen:

Oh let your shining orb grow dim,
Of Christ the mirror and the shield,
That I may gaze through you to Him,

See half the miracle revealed,
And in your seven hues behold
The Blue Man walking on the Sea;
The Green, beneath the summer tree,
Who called the children; then the Gold,
With palms; the Orange, flaring bold
With scourges; Purple in the garden
(As Greco saw): and then the Red
Torero (Him who took the toss
And rode the black horns of the cross—
But rose snow-silver from the dead!).

Campbell's Christianity, not surprisingly, was Mithraic in sentiment, as these verses show; Mithra, slayer of the bull, (whose cult closely resembled the Christian religion and was at one time, especially in the Rhône valley, its chief rival) being the god of soldiers and cattlemen.

Mithraic Emblems also contains one of the most interesting of Campbell's poems, *The Sling*. In *Taurine Provence*, a book that he wrote about this time, and which sets out to be a description of bullfighting in the South of France, but is in fact an exposition of Campbell's ideas and attitudes, a passage occurs which provides a prose gloss for the ideas behind *The Sling*:

> When consciousness becomes so shy and selfconscious that it tries to apologize for itself by studying itself in the collective third person, and explaining itself, it ceases to be consciousness. It begins to feed on secondhand experience and exists no longer in the first person. It becomes a spectator and ceases to be active. One's real existence is not what happens in the looking-glass; but science is all for looking in the looking-glass and it believes the looking-glass every time. It tries to supplant life by its reflection. It transfers experience from the first to the collective third person before it even deigns to consider it as experience; it is on account of this negative spirit, rather than any economic crisis, that our civilization is crumbling.

This passage, taken in conjunction with *The Sling*, is of special interest in view of Campbell's particular brand of

Romanticism, which might otherwise be dismissed as merely fanciful or at best belated. In his insistence upon the real i.e. first-hand experience of the facts, Campbell did not lose or abandon the loftier and spiritual elements contained in the Romantic vision. His Romanticism represents a serious development of the Romantic Movement of the nineteenth century because it embodies an anti-conventional romanticism. This is not merely the philosophy of the man of action, frontiersman, or landloper:

> Whose home's the Earth, and Everywhere his bed,
> A sheepskin saddle to his seat or head
> And Here and Now his permanent address.

For when Campbell stresses the necessity of physical, spiritual and intellectual self-reliance, it is because

> the world is not for Use,
> But is, to each, the fruit of his desire.

Thus, in the poem, Campbell apostrophizes the sling as the emblem of that independence which this, the simplest of weapons, confers on its user; a liberty and independence seen to be of the mind and soul no less than the body:

> Guarding my cattle on my native hill
> This was my talisman. Its charm was known
> High in the blue and aquiline ozone,
> And by my tireless armourer, the rill,
> Smoothing his pellets to my hand or eye:
> And how its meteors sang into the sky
> The eagles of the Berg remember still.

> I wore this herdsman's bracelet all day long:
> To me it meant 'Tomorrow' and 'Perhaps',
> The insults of Goliath, his collapse,
> Much fighting and (who knows?) a life of song . . .

Choosing my pebbles (to distinguish, free)
Ihad dispensed with numbers; finding how
Since Space was always Here as Time was Now,
Extent of either means a Fig to me;
To the whole field I can prefer a flower
And know that States are foundered by an hour
While centuries may groan to fell a tree.

By its cool guidance I unread my books
And learned, in spite of theories and charts,
Things have a nearer meaning to their looks
Than to their dead analyses in parts;
And how (for all the outfit be antique)
Our light is in our heads; and we can seek
The clearest information in our hearts.

While the best of Campbell is contained in his lyrics, epigrams, and translations, his two long poems *The Georgiad* and *Flowering Rifle* must be considered in any essay that pretends to discuss his work. Both are polemic satires written in heroic couplets (a metre which, for Campbell's sake, one could wish had never been invented).

The Georgiad, as the title indicates, is a satire on the 'Georgian' poets who were in vogue during the twenties. Many of them are now almost forgotten; but as Campbell remarked, the function of satire is to immortalize fools. Yet the real object of attack in *The Georgiad*, no less than in its model, the *Dunciad* of Alexander Pope, is not so much particular poets as mediocrity; the mediocrity of intellect and imagination propagated by the third-rate; the mediocrity in which the mediocre have themselves a vested interest. And it is not malice that prompts satires such as these on the dull and spurious (as the dull and spurious dearly love to believe) but outrage, the *saeva indignatio* of the genuine artist. But where Pope's wit flays like a scalpel, Campbell (like the eighteenth century satirist, Charles Churchill, with whom Campbell had really more in common than with Pope) hacks away with the blunter instrument of humour and ridicule. And this often deteriorates into boisterous abuse, partly because in his exuberance Campbell seldom failed to overdo things. Unlike Pope's, Campbell's mind was not sophisticate: he saw only primary colours, and did not distinguish between shades. As Vernon Watkins has remarked:

> He [Campbell] looked for a heroic world, and in poetry for all that was heroic and divine in the imagination. When he did not find it he protested violently . . . Poetically Roy Campbell was the very opposite of Rilke; or it is perhaps truer to say that his type of courage was the very opposite of the type Rilke possessed. The one was active, positive, crusading; the other passive, receptive, enduring. Rilke did not recognize enemies, but to Roy Campbell, who saw everything as black or white, they were as dramatically necessary as the dragon was to St. George.

But in *The Georgiad* Campbell indiscriminatingly lumps Robert Graves and Laura Riding with genuine nonentities, confusing them with his collective *bête noire*, the etiolated Bloomsbury fringe of arty

> intellectuals without intellect
> And sexless folk whose sexes intersect

Fabians, and 'progressive thinkers' who

> hatch Utopias from their dusty brains
> Which are but Hells, where endless boredom reigns—
> Middle-class Hells, built on a cheap, clean plan,
> Edens of abnegation, dread to scan,
> Founded upon a universal ban:
> For banned from thence is all that fires or thrills,
> Pain, vengeance, danger, or the clash of wills—
> So vastly greater is their fear of strife
> And hate of danger than their love of life.

Some of Campbell's comic exaggerations and burlesque

upbraidings of the poetasters of the time are great fun, but on the level of horseplay. The satire of *The Georgiad* too seldom attains the constructive wit of the derisive metaphor with which he caricatures the inadequate technique of a Georgian poet (J. C. Squire) in a passage that subtrudes, while it mocks, sound advice on the craft of verse:

> Nor at his football match is Squire more gay—
> Heart-rending verse describes funereal play;
> While swarming adjectives in idle ranks
> As dumb spectators, load the groaning planks,
> See the fat nouns, like porky forwards, sprawl
> Into a scrum that never heels the ball—
> A mass of moving bottoms like a sea,
> All fatter than his head, if that could be;
> While still attentive at their clumsy calves
> The adverbs pine away, dejected halves,
> The verbs stand useless by, like unfed threes,
> With trousers idly flapping in the breeze,
> And while they strike their arm-pits for some heat
> Or idly stamp their splayed trochaic feet,
> The two full-backs of alternating rhyme
> Walk sadly up and down to kill the time.

Campbell always saw himself as an individualist and non-conformer, a tramontane from another country and another century. The publication of *The Georgiad* did nothing to increase his popularity with the literary 'establishment' of the day, when so many members of it found themselves there subjected to his raucous belly-laughter. His isolation was intensified when the Spanish Civil War broke out in 1936. For some years he had been living with his family in Spain, in Toledo, where he added yet another avocation, that of horse-trader, to his already versatile list of gainful occupations. He and his family had become Roman Catholics. It was natural, then, that he should take the side of the rebels, who proclaimed themselves anti-communists and saviours of the Catholic Church. By this action Campbell made himself peculiarly invidious to his contemporaries in England. The Thirties had been a decade of unemployment and hunger-marches, of the rise of the Fascist tyrannies; to almost all writers and intellectuals the only hope then seemed to lie on the forces of socialism and even Communism. The emotional partisanship generated by the Spanish Civil War was intense; writers and poets like George Orwell and John Cornford volunteered to fight against Franco, and those who stayed at home wrote propaganda poems in favour of the workers' cause in Spain. When, in the middle of all this, Campbell produced *Flowering Rifle*, a long polemic poem about the Civil War in which he jeered at those 'pinks' and 'wowsers' who supported the 'Reds', he was fiercely attacked and his books boycotted.

Verse is, perhaps, the worst vehicle for argument, and, in particular, political argument. Like most political poems of that or any other time, *Flowering Rifle* is tedious, perhaps more tedious than most, on account of its enormous length (over 5,000 lines), its interminable tirades, and its savage vituperation, in which Campbell, in his political and emotional isolation, often seemed to lose all sense of proportion. This was the beginning of Campbell's famous feud with the young Thirties poets, W. H. Auden, Stephen Spender, Louis MacNeice and C. Day Lewis. Anything that smelt of a clique, a group, or a 'movement' in poetry was anathema to Campbell, quite apart from his disagreement with the left-wing political attitudes adumbrated by these four, whom he later satirized under the collective name of MacSpaunday in *Talking Bronco*, a poem that is in effect no more than an epigraph to *Flowering Rifle*.

When the Second World War broke out, Campbell volunteered to join the British Army, in which he served in the ranks, as a N.C.O., until he received an injury and was invalided out while a sergeant in the King's African Rifles. Much of his war service was spent in East Africa, and to this period belongs one of his finest sonnets:

Luis de Camoẽs

Camoẽs, alone, of all the lyric race,
Born in the black aurora of disaster,
Can look a common soldier in the face:
I find a comrade where I sought a master:
For daily, while the stinking crocodiles
Glide from the mangroves to the swampy shore,
He shares my awning in the dhow, he smiles,
And tells me he has lived it all before.
Through fire and shipwreck, pestilence and loss,
Led by the ignis fatuus of duty
To a dog's death—yet of his sorrows king—
He shouldered high his voluntary Cross
Wrestled his hardships into forms of beauty,
And taught his gorgon destinies to sing.

This appeared in *Talking Bronco*, his last collection of poems, in 1946.

In the post-war years, Campbell was less prolific with original poetry. Barring the sonnet quoted above and a dozen other scattered pieces, it was not of a quality equal to the best of his earlier work. The injuries he sustained during the war forced him to lead a more sedentary life, and perhaps this was one of the reasons. Action, with Campbell, was accessory to poetry; the one stimulated the other. When he left the Army, he came to live in London, where for some years he was a Talks Producer in the BBC and helped with the genesis of the Third Programme. In these years Campbell translated the poems of Baudelaire, and in 1951 published an autobiography, *Light on a Dark Horse*. This contains fine evocative chapters on his childhood in South Africa, but otherwise is not superior to *Broken Record*, an autobiographical fragment he had written seventeen years earlier. Both contain a number of anecdotes that are—to say the least—startling and fantastic; but as Campbell argued in *Broken Record*:

> I am so passionate a spectator of action that I have often found
> myself taking part in things which do not come the way of most

other poets, and a series of disjointed romantic adventures have been the result, some of which project into my imagination, but for that I can make no excuse, as my memory and imagination work as one; by force of recounting them they have assumed more elegant shapes, and I am not the one to bore you with a list of facts.

In 1952 Campbell left London for Portugal, where he had acquired a farm near Lisbon. Here he translated two novels by Eça de Quieroz, (one of which was *Cousin Bazilio*, the Portuguese equivalent of *Madame Bovary*) and several plays in verse by Lope de Vega and Tirso de Molina. His last prose book, a description of Portugal, appeared posthumously. Campbell's post-war years would seem to yield a meagre harvest of important work, were it not that some of his principal achievements belong to this period, namely his translations of the poems of Frederico Garcia Lorca and of St. John of the Cross.

VIII

It is seldom that translations are accorded the importance that should belong to them, either as part of the opus of an individual poet or for their vital share in the development of a literature. Yet, as Pound remarked, 'English literature lives on translation, it is fed by translation: every new heave is stimulated by translation, every allegedly great age is an age of translations'. Certainly the modern movement in English poetry has been distinguished, since 1910, by its number of notable translations from the poetry of other literatures. In this respect the nineteenth century, compared to the twentieth, seems curiously barren, its only major translations being those by Edward Fitzgerald, though perhaps one might include a few by Dante Gabriel Rossetti and H. W. Longfellow. Pound himself is indisputably the greatest translator of our time, but, after Pound, the laurel must go to Campbell, who, though not as apparently omnilingual or as consistently felicitous as Pound, made profitable raiding expeditions upon the poetry of half-a-dozen tongues. Campbell's versions of the poems of Baudelaire are not, however, particularly happy; but that was largely a result of the profound dissimilarity of temperament between the two. Where Campbell is simple, forceful, and direct, Baudelaire was sophisticate, elegant, subtle; in Campbell's translations it is as if the Parisian had been made to exchange his smoking-jacket and opium jar for cowboy leggings and a lariat. But if Campbell failed with Baudelaire he was conspicuously successful with Spanish and Portuguese poets, in particular Lorca and St. John of the Cross.

Campbell was peculiarly well qualified to translate Lorca. Himself a horseman and toreador, he was in singularly good position to understand and appreciate more intimately than most the equestrian culture and way of life in which Lorca's poems were rooted. Campbell's knowledge of Spain was of the kind obtained by living, rather than residing, in a country; by what used to be called 'going native'. His knowledge of Spain was of the inside looking out, rather than of the outside looking in. Nearly all the earlier translations of Lorca (at the time of the Spanish Civil War, in which he was killed, it was the fashion to translate him) ignored, or failed to bring out, a fundamental point: Lorca was almost entirely an oral poet, whose poems were designed to be listened to, not read. (Lorca's poems were famous all over Spain long before he allowed them to appear in print.) From these earlier translations, the singing quality, the rhyming and the verbal music that are integral to the original poems, was almost entirely absent. As a result, Lorca was often presented solely as a sort of midnight-oil pseudo-surrealist free-versifier; and, while many of his poems are in fact difficult, these translations indiscriminately invested them with a totally gratuitous obscurity. In contrast, Campbell's translations brought out the freshness, visual clarity, and the element of popular balladry, which is in Spain a living tradition, inherent in Lorca's work. Campbell and Lorca were both open-air poets, whose view of nature was unsentimental, utilitarian, and practical. (As Campbell wrote in his book on Lorca in which the translations are to be found: 'Nature leaves me cold, except as something to be dominated, confined, made to fructify, and loved, if at all, for the sake of the benefits it confers.') And Campbell's translations perform a further service in that they bring out not only the pace and energy of Lorca's poems but their gaiety, the unserious seriousness that is a hallmark of poetry. One has only to compare the translation of the refrain from *Romance Sonambulo*, from a well-known version published in the Thirties, with Campbell's rendering:

> Green, how I love you, green.
> Green wind, green branches.
> The ship upon the sea.
> And the horse in the mountain.
>   (*Spender & Gili*)

> Green, O green, how deeply green!
> Green the wind and green the bough,
> The ship upon the waters seen,
> The horse upon the mountain's brow.
>   (*Campbell*)

Unfortunately the best of Campbell's translations from Lorca are too long to quote, and lose much when not given in full. But one of the shorter pieces, *The Song of the Horseman*, is reproduced below to illustrate how Campbell recreated in English some of the auditory effect of the original poem, in which the vowels and consonants are so ordered as to suggest the muffed hoofbeats of the horse:

> Cordoba.
> Remote and lonely.

Jet-black mare and full round moon,
With olives in my saddle-bags,
Although I know the road so well
I shall not get to Cordoba.

Across the plain, across the wind,
Jet-black mare and full red moon,
Death is gazing down upon me,
Down from the towers of Cordoba,

Ay! The road so dark and long
Ay! My mare so tired yet brave.
Death is waiting for me there
Before I get to Cordoba.

Cordoba.
Remote and lonely.

One would have thought Campbell, the pugnacious satirist and polemist, would be the last person capable of translating, and translating miraculously, the ecstatic lyrics of a mystic and a visionary. Yet his version of the poems of St. John of the Cross is one of the most admired translations of our time. The most astonishing thing about Campbell's rendering of these profound yet limpid lyrics of ineffable experience, is the consistently inspired poetic recreation that he made of his original:

BRIDEGROOM
    Turn, Ringdove, and alight
The wounded stag above
The slope is now in sight
Fanned by the wind and freshness of your flight.

BRIDE
My love's the mountain range,
The valleys each with solitary grove,
The islands far and strange,
The streams and sounds that range,
The whistling of the lovesick winds that rove.

It was not simply his basic sympathy (born of affinity and intimate knowledge of the people) with the Spanish temperament that enabled him to interpret St. John of the Cross with even more sureness and authority than in the case of Lorca. There was a quality of sensuousness in Campbell's own verse, which turned out to be an invaluable asset when he came to remake in English the poems of St. John. The truth is, Campbell had a magnanimous simplicity, a fervour, and, strange as this may seem in the face of the arrogance he paraded, a humility, upon which he drew with profit in order to match the intensity of these qualities in the work of the Spanish rhapsodist. This may be seen in the most famous of his translations from St. John of the Cross, his version of *En Una Noche Oscura:*

> Upon a gloomy night,
> With all my cares to loving ardours flushed,
> (O venture of delight!)
> With nobody in sight
> I went abroad when all my house was hushed.

> In safety, in disguise,
> In darkness up the secret stair I crept,
> (O happy enterprise!)
> Concealed from other eyes
> When all my house at length in silence slept.

> Upon that lucky night
> In secrecy, inscrutable to sight,
> I went without discerning
> And with no other light
> Except for that which in my heart was burning.

> It lit and led me through
> More certain than the light of noonday clear
> To where One waited near
> Whose presence well I knew,
> There where no other presence might appear.

Oh night that was my guide!
Oh darkness dearer than the morning's pride,
Oh night that joined the lover
To the beloved bride,
Transfiguring them each into the other.

Within my flowering breast
Which only for himself entire I save
He sank into his rest
And all my gifts I gave
Lulled by the airs with which the cedars wave.

Over the ramparts fanned
While the fresh wind was fluttering his tresses,
With his serenest hand
My neck he wounded, and
Suspended every sense with its caresses.

Lost to myself I stayed
My face upon my lover having laid
From all endeavour ceasing:
And all my cares releasing
Threw them amongst the lilies there to fade.

IX

No contemporary poet involved himself in so many
explosive, and often vacuous, feuds as Roy Campbell. In
most of them there was an element of sublime burlesque,
rather like the exploits of Quixote which are both noble
and ridiculous. The extreme simplicity and romanticism of
his nature were the arms of the crusading angle from which
he approached any question or dispute. Once committed,
he did not desert his loyalties; but the bargain was not
reciprocal.

Campbell was all his life an outsider. For him the experience of that double exile, felt with varying intensity by all

those who came from a raw country to live in the old world, was crucial. Among colonials he was a European and among Europeans a colonial; among cowboys a poet and among poets a cowboy. This probably strengthened out of proportion the 'restive steer' side of his character. Thus, it became more and more his nature not to align himself with a minority against a majority or vice versa but to be the dissident among the minority. When he came to England from South Africa after the first world war, 'Georgian' poetry was strongly entrenched and 'modern' verse a subject of ridicule. It was to the avant-garde minority, led by Eliot and Pound, that Campbell aligned himself, but, at the same time, he was, so far as style went, the dissident of that minority; for his own verse was apparently as 'traditional', though much more tough and muscular, as that of the Georgian 'Squirearchy' he satirized. Then, when aesthetes made *épater la bourgeoisie* their business, Campbell made it his to *épater les bohemiens*. In an illiberal society, South Africa, Campbell got himself into hot water by attacking the colour bar; in England, by airing prejudices, indefensible to liberal intellectuals, against 'homos', 'Reds', and 'Yids'.

He once said to me: 'I place friendship above art', and, from what I knew of him personally, it was transparent that he also placed it well above those reiterated declarations of intolerance, for among his friends he counted dozens of people in his three condemned categories. The fact is nobody had a more catholic or contradictory assortment of friends of so many diverse races, colours, creeds, and political tenets, or from so many varying walks of life. In one way, this was no more than a reflection of Campbell's multiple interests and accomplishments, and in another a consequence of his openhearted, almost childlike, love of human beings, especially those who shared in one form or another his enormous gusto in living.

I first met Campbell one damp night in the spring of 1946, in one of the Soho pubs which were then the rendezvous of poets, painters, musicians, editors of little reviews, kings of Poland, and the fabulous grizzling survivors of l'*entre deux guerres* Bloomsbury and Montparnasse. Coming into its saloon bar, I found it crammed with the usual assortment of warriors of various forces and nations as well as the regular clientele. That particular wet evening, having dug my way to the bar through the steaming uniforms of allied servicemen, I found myself wedged opposite a battered imperial face, cold eyes and a wide cruel-looking mouth set under a cockaded slouch hat, the gorgeous headgear of the King's African Rifles. It was Roy Campbell. He was drinking with Tambimuttu, the Ceylonese editor of *Poetry London*, who took the opportunity of introducing two South Africans to each other. In the course of the next few years I came to know Campbell well, and to discover that the huge friendly man, with the limp and the unbenevolent-seeming mouth, was almost the exact reverse of the truculent *persona* he loved to project in his writing.

It is true that Campbell hated, but it was usually in the abstract; like H. G. Wells, he would have had to admit, 'I always get so amiable when I *meet* a man'. The longer I knew him the stronger the impression I received of a great and fundamental gentleness beneath a superficial truculence, though this may appear absurd to those who take at its face value the ferocity of his polemic satire and the violence of his legend. Campbell's ruggedness was theatrical; a thing put on; the apparent vainglory and braggadocio, with which he embroidered his exploits, part of a mask behind which he hid an actual and active humility that touched one more than the assumed modesty or silent pride worn by less naïve personalities. I once made a disparaging remark about one of the Thirties poets he had satirized in *Talking Bronco*, whom Campbell had since come to know personally. 'X——— is a very shy man, not supercilious as you think', he retorted. 'I used to hate him and push him out of my way—but I was more at fault than he.' And it was typical of Campbell's kindliness and generosity that, at our second encounter, he should extend to me, an unknown deaf youth with whom he could communicate only by the laborious expedient of writing down every word he wanted to say, a standing invitation to visit him on Sunday afternoons at his home in Campden Grove.

Campbell had a gift for surrealistic ridicule and was the natural enemy of anything that smacked to him of privilege, of the 'Establishment', or of a coterie; of any sort of drybone academism, deathshead puritanism, and highbrow spoof; in particular of anything that seemed to him a turning of the back on enjoyment and life. In this, and other, respects he and his friend Dylan Thomas were much alike; they shared the same magnanimity of spirit, plus a rustic mistrust of the urban and urbane.

After Campbell resigned his post as a producer in the BBC (a job he enjoyed, though in moments of exasperation he would say, 'if all the brains of all the producers of the Third Programme were made of dynamite, tied together and set off, it wouldn't blow the cap off a commissionaire's head') I saw less of him. He took a farm in Portugal; and thereafter we met spasmodically, usually around Christmas time, which he spent in England as a rule. Almost the last time I saw him was in 1954 when he invited my wife and me to spend Christmas with him. At dinner, Campbell was in splendid vein, telling gargantuan stories of disgraceful mishaps; but what I recollect best is one of those small incidents that sometimes provide a clue to character. I was trying to crack a walnut with the usual implement when Campbell took it from me and, placing it in the massive crook of his elbow, set his biceps to work to split it in two. He went through a formidable pantomine of effort, veins bulging from his forehead and the sweat pouring down, while the rest of us watched appalled, wondering if he was going to burst a blood-vessel. After thirty excruciating seconds of terrifying exertion, he produced the nut neatly cracked. Overwhelmed by his spectacular demonstration I thought, 'My word, the old man's even stronger than he says he is'.

But, later, he took me aside and, after swearing me to secrecy, explained it was a parlour trick (you hold the nut in a certain way so that the slightest pressure cracks it). Then it struck me that Campbell's more grandiose feats of physical prowess, of which he loved to boast, had about them the same element —part bluff, part illusion, and part joke—which is not to say they were phoney, but that for him these feats did not have the importance he pretended to attach to them. Thus, in his autobiography, he has written much of his skills with horse and gun and of his deeds in the bullring but says very little about his own poetry. In this I see the operation of a profound, even a perverse, humility which led Campbell to cyclopean bragging of qualities and talents that were not specifically his or, if they were, of small importance compared to his true gift. All good poets wear a mask, and Campbell had several—toreador, cowboy, and old sweat. The danger is that the features behind the mask may become moulded to it. That this nemesis overtook Campbell the wilder notes appended to the posthumous second volume of his *Collected Poems* perhaps bear witness.

The last time I saw Campbell was some months before his death. He was to fly to Portugal the next day and I had gone to 'The Catherine Wheel' to say goodbye. When I arrived at the pub he was not there, but his wife and daughter and a dozen or more friends sat waiting for him in an alcove in the saloon bar. Everyone was worried about Campbell's health; a week before a doctor had diagnosed a diabetic condition. That night Campbell was very late in getting to the pub. We were wondering if he was going to appear at all when the swing door opened and the old man came in, huge and rolling, his black Cordoba at an angle over his whitening sideburns, and great torso wrapped in a magnificent cape. He was leaning on a silver-headed malacca, his whole appearance flamboyant and fabulous, a shark among goldfish; ex-sergeant, poet, and toreador, grinning like a schoolboy. Before we could get up to welcome him, an extraordinary thing happened: everyone

in the pub spontaneously rose to his feet, though only those
who were waiting in the alcove may have known to whom
or for what the involuntary ovation had been given.

X

Roy Campbell was killed in a car crash in Portugal on
St. George's Day, 1957. It is not easy, so soon after his death,
to assess the work of one so uniquely placed and composed
of so many contradictory qualities. Campbell was respon-
sible for no technical innovations in verse; and it would
be true to say that he left the English language where he
found it. He achieved nothing new in his handling of it,
his work made no apparent difference to the development
of contemporary English poetry, or not the kind of
difference that can be assessed by the test of the comparative
analytic criticism now fashionable. Yet much the same
complaint could be made of George Crabbe, who, in the
age of Wordsworth, contributed nothing to the literary
revolution of the time; for all that, Crabbe remains a
poet we cannot ignore. And this is the case with Campbell,
who is not to be fitted in as a neat cog in the machine which
future literary historians will inevitably construct and label
'The Development of English Literature in the Twentieth
Century'. As Robert Graves has warned: 'Literature is a
cumulative tradition: authentic poetry is a number of
unrelated events, or poems.' That Campbell was an authentic poet there can be no doubt; that he was an 'unrelated
event' will probably bother posterity less than his contemporaries. But, in another and more intangible sense,
Campbell exercised an influence extraneous to the actual
body of work he left behind him. As Vernon Watkins has
pointed out, 'he maintained a singularly consistent role as
inspired campaigner and champion of the under-dog', and,
like Dr. Johnson, Campbell was in the habit of champion-

ing what he considered the real, rather than the obvious or currently fashionable under-dog. Further he affirmed, in his life and in his work, the validity of the poetic vocation, its serious character and its morality of delight, in an age when its existence is either denied or, by pedants and cultural organisations, polluted by various subtle and well-meant forms of standardization and commercialization. 'There are no substitutes for morality, honour, and loyalty, either in themselves (as we are so painfully learning) or as the substance of poetry.' In this sense Campbell was a Don Quixote whose courage and valour were dedicated to a vanished ethic, and whose values only seem comic or insane in the measure that the world is debased.

> For all the outfit be antique
> Our light is in our heads: and we can seek
> The clearest information in our hearts.

ROY CAMPBELL

A Select Bibliography

(Place of publication London, unless stated otherwise)

Collected Editions:

SONS OF THE MISTRAL (1941).

—selected poems in the Sesame series.

COLLECTED POEMS, Vol. I (1949), Vol. II (1957), Vol. III (Translations) (1960).

Separate Works:

I. Verse

THE FLAMING TERRAPIN (1924).

THE WAYZGOOSE (1928).

ADAMASTOR (1930).

THE GUM TREES (1930)—a single poem in the Ariel Poets series.

THE GEORGIAD (1931).

POEMS (1931).

CHOOSING A MAST (1931)—a single poem in the Ariel Poems series.

POMEGRANATES (1932).

FLOWERING REEDS (1933).

MITHRAIC EMBLEMS (1936).

FLOWERING RIFLE: A POEM FROM THE BATTLEFIELDS OF SPAIN (1939).

TALKING BRONCO (1946).

NATIVITY (1954)—a single poem in the Ariel Poems series.

II. Prose

TAURINE PROVENCE (1932).

BROKEN RECORD (1934). *Autobiography.*

LIGHT ON A DARK HORSE (1951). *Autobiography.*

LORCA: AN APPRECIATION OF HIS POETRY (1952). *Criticism.*

PORTUGAL (1957).

III. Translations

THREE PLAYS BY HELGE KROG (1934)

—includes *The Copy, Happily Ever After,* and *Triad.*

THE POEMS OF ST. JOHN OF THE CROSS (1951).

THE POEMS OF BAUDELAIRE (1952).

COUSIN BAZILIO, by E. de Quieroz (1953).

THE CITY AND THE MOUNTAINS, by E. de Quieroz (1955).

THE CLASSIC THEATRE, Vol. III. New York (1959)

—contains verse plays translated from the Spanish.

NOSTALGIA, a collection of poems by J. Paço D'Arcos (1960).

WRITERS AND THEIR WORK

General Editor: BONAMY DOBRÉE

The first 55 issues in the Series appeared under the General Editorship of T. O. BEACHCROFT

Sixteenth Century and Earlier:
FRANCIS BACON: J. Max Patrick
CHAUCER: Nevill Coghill
ENGLISH MARITIME WRITING:
    Hakluyt to Cook: Oliver Warner
MALORY: M. C. Bradbrook
MARLOWE: Philip Henderson
SIDNEY: Kenneth Muir
SKELTON: Peter Green
SPENSER: Rosemary Freeman

Seventeenth Century:
SIR THOMAS BROWNE: Peter Green
BUNYAN: Henry Talon
CAVALIER POETS: Robin Skelton
DONNE: Frank Kermode
DRYDEN: Bonamy Dobrée
HERRICK: John Press
HOBBES: T. E. Jessop
BEN JONSON: J. B. Bamborough
LOCKE: Maurice Cranston
ANDREW MARVELL: John Press
MILTON: E. M. W. Tillyard
SHAKESPEARE: C. J. Sisson
SHAKESPEARE: EARLY COMEDIES:
    Derek Traversi
SHAKESPEARE: GREAT TRAGEDIES
    Kenneth Muir
THREE METAPHYSICAL POETS:
    Margaret Willy
IZAAK WALTON: Margaret Bottrall

Eighteenth Century:
BERKELEY: T. E. Jessop
BLAKE: Kathleen Raine
BOSWELL: P. A. W. Collins
BURKE: T. E. Utley
BURNS: David Daiches
COWPER: N. Nicholson
CRABBE: R. L. Brett
DEFOE: J. R. Sutherland
FIELDING: John Butt
GIBBON: C. V. Wedgwood

GOLDSMITH: A. Norman Jeffares
GRAY: R. W. Ketton-Cremer
HYMNS: Arthur Pollard
JOHNSON: S. C. Roberts
POPE: Ian Jack
RICHARDSON: R. F. Brissenden
SHERIDAN: W. A. Darlington
SMOLLETT: Laurence Brander
STEELE, ADDISON AND THEIR
  PERIODICAL ESSAYS:
    A. R. Humphreys
STERNE: D. W. Jefferson
SWIFT: J. Middleton Murry
HORACE WALPOLE: Hugh Honour
CHRISTOPHER SMART:
    Geoffrey Grigson

Nineteenth Century:
MATTHEW ARNOLD: Kenneth Allott
JANE AUSTEN: S. Townsend Warner
THE BRONTË SISTERS:
    Phyllis Bentley
BROWNING: John Bryson
SAMUEL BUTLER: G. D. H. Cole
BYRON: Herbert Read
CARLYLE: David Gascoyne
LEWIS CARROLL: Derek Hudson
COLERIDGE: Kathleen Raine
DICKENS: K. J. Fielding
GEORGE ELIOT: Lettice Cooper
ENGLISH TRAVELLERS IN THE NEAR
  EAST: Robin Fedden
FITZGERALD: Joanna Richardson
MRS. GASKELL: Miriam Allott
GISSING: A. C. Ward
THOMAS HARDY: R. A. Scott-James
HAZLITT: J. B. Priestley
G. M. HOPKINS: Geoffrey Grigson
T. H. HUXLEY: William Irvine
KEATS: Edmund Blunden
LAMB: Edmund Blunden
LANDOR: G. Rostrevor Hamilton

MACAULAY: G. R. Potter
JOHN STUART MILL: M. Cranston
WILLIAM MORRIS: P. Henderson
NEWMAN: J. M. Cameron
PATER: Iain Fletcher
ROSSETTI: Oswald Doughty
RUSKIN: Peter Quennell
SIR WALTER SCOTT: Ian Jack
SHELLEY: Stephen Spender
R. L. STEVENSON: G. B. Stern
SWINBURNE: H. J. C. Grierson
TENNYSON: F. L. Lucas
THACKERAY: Laurence Brander
TROLLOPE: Hugh Sykes Davies
OSCAR WILDE: James Laver
WORDSWORTH: Helen Darbyshire

JOHN GALSWORTHY: R. H. Mottra
ROBERT GRAVES: M. Seymour Smit
GRAHAM GREENE: Francis Wyndha
A. E. HOUSMAN: Ian Scott-Kilvert
ALDOUS HUXLEY: Jocelyn Brooke
HENRY JAMES: Michael Swan
JAMES JOYCE: J. I. M. Stewart
RUDYARD KIPLING: B. Dobrée
D. H. LAWRENCE: Kenneth Young
C. DAY LEWIS: Clifford Dyment
WYNDHAM LEWIS: E. W. F. Tomli
KATHERINE MANSFIELD: Ian Gordo
JOHN MASEFIELD: L. A. G. Strong
SOMERSET MAUGHAM: J. Brophy
EDWIN MUIR: J. C. Hall
J. MIDDLETON MURRY: Philip Mair
GEORGE ORWELL: Tom Hopkinson
POETS OF THE 1939-45 WAR:
R. N. Curre

Twentieth Century:

W. H. AUDEN: Richard Hoggart
HILAIRE BELLOC: Renée Haynes
ARNOLD BENNETT: F. Swinnerton
EDMUND BLUNDEN: Alec M. Hardie
ELIZABETH BOWEN: Jocelyn Brooke
JOYCE CARY: Walter Allen
G. K. CHESTERTON: C. Hollis
WINSTON CHURCHILL: John Connell
R. G. COLLINGWOOD:
E. W. F. Tomlin
L. COMPTON-BURNETT:
Pamela Hansford Johnson
JOSEPH CONRAD: Oliver Warner
WALTER DE LA MARE: K. Hopkins
NORMAN DOUGLAS: Ian Greenlees
T. S. ELIOT: M. C. Bradbrook
FORD MADOX FORD: Kenneth Young
E. M. FORSTER: Rex Warner
CHRISTOPHER FRY: Derek Stanford

J. B. PRIESTLEY: Ivor Brown
HERBERT READ: Francis Berry
BERTRAND RUSSELL: Alan Dorwar
BERNARD SHAW: A. C. Ward
EDITH SITWELL: John Lehmann
OSBERT SITWELL: Roger Fulford
C. P. SNOW: William Cooper
LYTTON STRACHEY:
R. A. Scott-Jame
DYLAN THOMAS: G. S. Fraser
G. M. TREVELYAN: J. H. Plumb
WAR POETS: 1914-18:
Edmund Blunder
EVELYN WAUGH: Christopher Holli
H. G. WELLS: Montgomery Belgion
CHARLES WILLIAMS:
John Heath-Stubbs
VIRGINIA WOOLF: Bernard Blackstone
W. B. YEATS: G. S. Fraser

In Preparation:

Sixteenth Century:
SIR THOMAS WYATT: Sergio Baldi

Nineteenth Century:
DISRAELI: Paul Bloomfield